It Is Raining

Kelly Doudna

Consulting Editor Monica Marx, M.A./Reading Specialist

ABDO
Publishing Company

Published by SandCastle™, an imprint of ABDO Publishing Company, 4940 Viking Drive, Edina, Minnesota 55435.

Printed in the United States.

Credits
Edited by: Pam Price
Curriculum Coordinator: Nancy Tuminelly
Cover and Interior Design and Production: Mighty Media
Photo Credits: Comstock, Corbis Images, Digital Vision, PhotoDisc, Stockbyte

Library of Congress Cataloging-in-Publication Data

Doudna, Kelly, 1963-
    It is raining / Kelly Doudna.
        p. cm. -- (The weather)
    Includes index.
    Summary: A very simple introduction to the characteristics of rain.
    ISBN 1-57765-774-8
        1. Rain and rainfall--Juvenile literature. [1. Rain and rainfall.] I. Title.

QC924.7 .D68 2002
551.57'7--dc21

2002018367

SandCastle™ books are created by a professional team of educators, reading specialists, and content developers around five essential components that include phonemic awareness, phonics, vocabulary, text comprehension, and fluency. All books are written, reviewed, and leveled for guided reading, early intervention reading, and Accelerated Reader® programs and designed for use in shared, guided, and independent reading and writing activities to support a balanced approach to literacy instruction.

Let Us Know

After reading the book, SandCastle would like you to tell us your stories about reading. What is your favorite page? Was there something hard that you needed help with? Share the ups and downs of learning to read. We want to hear from you! To get posted on the ABDO Publishing Company Web site, send us email at:

sandcastle@abdopub.com

SandCastle Level: Beginning

What is rain?

Rain is drops of water.

Raindrops form
inside clouds.

Light rain is a shower.

Heavy rain is a downpour.

Rain makes the streets wet.

A little extra rain
makes puddles.

ROAD CLOSED

PUBLIC WORKS

A lot of extra rain floods roads.

Rainbows form if
the sun is out while
it rains.

Sue and Deb have
an umbrella to
keep them dry.

Do you?

Picture Index

clouds, p. 7

rainbows, p. 19

drops, p. 5

umbrella, p. 21

puddles, p. 15

water, p. 5

rain, pp. 3, 5, 9, 11,
13, 15, 17

Match the words to the pictures

clouds   puddles

drops   umbrella

23

About SandCastle™

A professional team of educators, reading specialists, and content developers created the SandCastle™ series to support young readers as they develop reading skills and strategies and increase their general knowledge. The SandCastle™ series has four levels that correspond to early literacy development in young children. The levels are provided to help teachers and parents select the appropriate books for young readers.

Emerging Readers
(no flags)

Beginning Readers
(1 flag)

Transitional Readers
(2 flags)

Fluent Readers
(3 flags)

These levels are meant only as a guide. All levels are subject to change.

To see a complete list of SandCastle™ books and other nonfiction titles from ABDO Publishing Company, visit **www.abdopub.com** or contact us at:

4940 Viking Drive, Edina, Minnesota 55435 • 1-800-800-1312 • fax: 1-952-831-1632